D0358460

the saatchi gift to the arts council collection

the saatchi gift
to the arts council collection

Arts Council Collection

the saatchi gift to the arts council collection

Designed by Kate Stephens
Production coordinated by Uwe Kraus GmbH
Printed in Italy

Published by Hayward Gallery Publishing, London SE1 8XX
© The South Bank Centre 2000

Quotations and biographies compiled by Ann Jones, Julia Risness
and Isobel Johnstone
Texts © Isobel Johnstone and the artists 2000
Images © the artists 2000
with the exception of
Mark Francis: © the artist, Maureen Paley Interim Art 2000
Melanie Manchot: © the artist, courtesy Rhodes + Mann

The publisher has made every effort to contact all copyright holders.
If proper acknowledgement has not been made, we ask copyright
holders to contact the publisher.

ISBN 1 85332 207 5

All rights reserved. No part of this publication may be produced,
stored in a retrieval system or transmitted in any form or by any
means without the prior permission in writing of the publisher.

This catalogue is not intended to be used for authentication or
related purposes. The South Bank Board Limited accepts no liability
for any errors or omissions which the catalogue may inadvertently
contain.

Hayward Gallery Publishing titles are distributed outside North and
South America and Canada by Cornerhouse Publications, 70 Oxford
Street, Manchester M1 5NH (tel 0161 200 1503; fax 0161 200
1504; email: publications@cornerhouse.org).

I greatly admire the Arts Council Collection and its ongoing support over many years for young artists. No institution does more than the Hayward Gallery on behalf of the Arts Council, to curate touring exhibitions and loans to the nation's galleries and museums. The gift will give these artists a chance to be seen more widely across the country.

Charles Saatchi February 1999

In February 1999 Charles Saatchi donated 100 works of art to the Arts Council Collection. This book presents the gift in its entirety. It celebrates artists whose activities have enriched British life of late and welcomes their work to a base from which it will be widely available for loan. Charles Saatchi, an enthusiastic supporter of British art of the 90s, has helped make 'Britart' a subject of popular interest and enjoyment. The Arts Council Collection welcomes this special endowment. It has provided an unexpected enhancement of the Collection at an extraordinary point for the visual arts in Britain.

We should like to thank Charles Saatchi for entrusting these works to the Arts Council Collection. His patience and generosity during discussions about the gift simplified and smoothed every aspect of the accession process. Our profound gratitude also goes to the artists, who have been unfailingly flexible about this transfer of ownership, helpful in the completion of its formalities, and who have additionally provided new information and quotations for this publication. Many private London galleries have, as ever, been very accommodating, and we thank them for their support. It has been a particular pleasure to work with the Saatchi Gallery whose staff could not have been more obliging or efficient; and we are especially indebted to Jenny Blyth, Curator, Nigel Hurst, Assistant Curator, and Linda Copperwheat, Archivist. We also extend our thanks to Momart, which has been responsible for storage of the works of art prior to loan.

Very special thanks go to David Sylvester, a longstanding friend of the Collection, Hayward Gallery and Arts Council, for his role in stimulating the first discussions between Charles Saatchi and ourselves. We are grateful too to the representatives of the Arts Council of England and the Hayward Gallery who made it possible to reach formal agreement on the gift. In this regard, thanks are due to Gerry Robinson, Chairman of the Arts Council of England, and to Elliott Bernerd, Chairman of SBC. We also wish to thank the staff of the Hayward Gallery responsible for realizing this publication and for handling the works: Isobel Johnstone, Ann Jones, Kate Bell, Lise Connellan, Ella O'Halloran, Jill Constantine, Christie Coutin, Ryan Rodgers, Peter Stiff and Julia Risness. Kate Stephens, a frequent partner on publications relating to the Collection, is to be congratulated once again for her fine design.

Susan Ferleger Brades, Director, Hayward Gallery
Marjorie Allthorpe-Guyton, Director, Visual Arts, Arts Council of England
February 2000

foreword

When Charles Saatchi offered to give 100 works of art to the Arts Council Collection the news was received by the Hayward Gallery and the Arts Council of England with excitement and surprise. Most public collections in this country have at their heart major donations from private individuals but this was never the case with the Arts Council Collection. The Collection has occasionally been given a work by an artist as an expression of gratitude for an exhibition organised, initially, by the Arts Council and, in later years, by the Hayward Gallery, or been left a small bequest by someone aware of its activities. The scale of this offer was unprecedented. The donor, moreover, was not uncontroversial. In the ten years that he has focused on collecting contemporary British art, Charles Saatchi has attained exceptional public awareness of his activities.

Since opening a large gallery to display his collection in north London, Charles Saatchi has informed and transformed public perception of modern and contemporary work from abroad and in Britain.[1] A partner in M & C Saatchi[2] would inevitably have distinct advantages as a promoter, but it is for the daring and extent of his acquisitions of contemporary British work that Charles Saatchi is most notable, and it is a part of this aspect of his collection which makes up the present gift.

The generation that emerged after the economic collapse of the mid-1980s succeeded in raising the temperature of British art, at home and internationally. Tracey Emin, Adam Chodzko, John Frankland, Damien Hirst, Gary Hume, Richard Patterson, Hadrian Pigott, Fiona Rae and Rachel Whiteread, among others, produced an array of works that could surprise and shock as well as delight viewers. The 'low temperature' of much of twentieth-century British art until then may well, as Richard Shone has suggested,[3] have been due to an inability of artists to commit fully to Modernism or to develop a strong indigenous strain. As art historical perceptions of artistic progress have relaxed in the last twenty-five years, individual British achievements have increasingly been recognized and acclaimed abroad, and sometimes sooner than in Britain itself. Francis Bacon, Lucian Freud, Richard Hamilton, Howard Hodgkin, Bridget Riley, Richard Long, Tony Cragg and Richard Deacon, among others, are universally respected. There is a seriousness about much of their work which encourages admiration from connoisseurs and the establishment; the work of certain Young British Artists, who are now dubbed 'YBAs', excites stronger reactions and touches a popular nerve.

Comparison is often made with the 1960s when Anthony Caro and other New Generation sculptors, and the Pop artists, notably David Hockney, became symbols for new life styles in a period of sexual liberation and financial optimism. It was smart then to be British, and Chelsea, Carnaby Street and the Beatles combined in a heady mix. Whatever has contributed to the success of the YBAs, be it brave dealers, entrepreneurial and self-promoting artists, diversified art teaching, the influence of Goldsmiths College, business sponsorship, or the concentration of a mass of artists in east and south-east London, it is difficult to divorce the phenomenon from the name of Charles Saatchi.[4]

raising the temperature 100°

Private collectors can indulge individual taste, back hunches and move quickly; galleries in the public sector are rightly limited by controls which make them answerable to committees and trustees. Public collections must consider how a proposed new acquisition will fit with existing holdings and take a long-term view. Decisions can seldom be made quickly (a real difficulty when buying work that is in demand) and, once made, are irrevocable as few public collections can de-accession. Charles Saatchi recently commented: 'I buy for the sheer pleasure of mounting interesting shows. Throughout history there have always been those poor souls who have taken the step beyond collecting, who have wanted to create temples to their taste and display their pet treasures to a wide public. People like that soon stop seeing themselves as collectors, and become instead commissioning editors. If I wasn't lucky enough to have such a beautiful gallery to work with I'd certainly have effectively stopped collecting years ago.' When he sells art, as Jenny Blyth (Curator of the Saatchi Gallery) has explained, it is in order to buy more art and to finance his gallery. In addition, as in the case of the Christie's auction in December 1998, he has used the proceeds to create ongoing scholarships at five London art schools and give commissions to artists. Charles Saatchi's decision to give so many works to the Arts Council Collection was taken because the Collection could help to maintain their visibility, and artists would benefit from being in a national collection.

The interests and aims of the Arts Council Collection are not, in fact, so far removed from those of this benefactor. Set up for touring when the Arts Council of Great Britain was established just after the Second World War, the Arts Council Collection was used to show contemporary British art outside London, which was then, as it still is, the main centre for innovative activity. The largest loan collection of its kind in the world, the Collection now contains 7000 works of art, 3500 of which are sculptures, paintings, mixed media, installation and video, 2000 of which are photographs and 1500 artists' prints. It is lent extensively to exhibitions organised by museums and galleries as well as forming the basis, each year, for several National Touring Exhibitions, as the Arts Council's touring service is now called. Like the Collection, this is now administered by the Hayward Gallery in London on behalf of the (renamed) Arts Council of England. Although the Collection has no permanent gallery in which to show work, parts of it are occasionally shown in the Hayward Gallery. It is most often seen all around Britain, where works are on long-term loan to museums and galleries as well as to a wide range of public buildings, such as colleges and hospitals. In this way people can encounter art in the course of a normal working day or in their leisure hours.

Inevitably slower off the mark than Charles Saatchi in purchasing many of the new British artists in the early 1990s, the Arts Council Collection was nonetheless probably quicker than most other public collections. It already had original and unique works by many artists who were also favoured by Charles Saatchi and selected for *Sensation*, the exhibition of new British art from the Saatchi Collection that was

raising the temperature 100°

shown at the Royal Academy in 1997. Among these were Peter Davies, Tracey Emin, Mona Hatoum, Damien Hirst, Gary Hume, Michael Landy, Alain Miller, Chris Ofili, Richard Patterson, Simon Patterson, Fiona Rae, James Rielly, Gavin Turk, Mark Wallinger, Gillian Wearing and Rachel Whiteread.[5] While the gift itself does not include works by these artists, fourteen other artists whose work was shown in *Sensation* are represented in it. In all, of the sixty-three artists that were included in the gift, thirty were already represented in the Collection.

The Collection shares Charles Saatchi's commitment to young artists and buys a wide range of new works. At first, purchases were made with an element of historical gap-filling but the focus soon concentrated on contemporary work with an emphasis on emerging younger artists. Purchasing resources have always been modest (the present annual allocation is £152,600, supplemented occasionally and most recently by generous grants for specific sculptures from The Henry Moore Foundation and the National Art Collections Fund). Over the years it has evolved a way of purchasing that maintains accountability and yet gives freedom to move quickly as well as scope for the enthusiasms of individual purchasers, thus avoiding the pitfalls of committee buying or entrenched curating. Six individuals, usually an artist, a writer and a curator, the Director of the Arts Council of England's Visual Arts Department, the Director of the Hayward Gallery and the Curator of the Collection, purchase for eighteen months, after which a new group of outside purchasers is appointed to allow a change of views. The Collection buys work by living British artists or artists living in Britain. It is not able to acquire student work, and purchasers generally spend less time visiting college diploma shows than Charles Saatchi.

Having been offered art of such breadth and diversity, the Collection had to think about its potential impact. Could it be used in the same way as the rest of the Collection? Would we be able to show it as widely as hoped? Would it give too much emphasis to a certain kind of work? The overlap in artists and the fact that many others on the gift list had been under consideration but not yet bought answered one question. The success of a recent National Touring Exhibition show, *Here to Stay*, which featured new Collection purchases, indicated that more work of this kind was in demand. Some of the pieces offered were too close to existing examples in the Collection. A very few dealt with subjects that might cause offence and which we would be unable to show in places to which the public have unimpeded access. In other cases, too many works by the same artist would have jeopardized their chance of being purchased again in the near future. After a frank and free discussion with Charles Saatchi, alternatives were offered and accepted.

The physical implications of storage and handling were also addressed. As a touring and loan resource, the Collection has always had to consider the ease with which works can be stored, transported and displayed. The gift included several logistically complicated works, including two major examples by artists who have been influential in recent years, and it was impossible to resist them. One was by Richard Wilson, whose *20:50* of 1987, an installation comprising a walk-in tank of sump oil, is one of the most popular exhibits at the Saatchi Gallery. His *High Rise*, 1989, consisting of a glass greenhouse and two insect-o-cutors, needs to be installed within the wall of a gallery. The other, by Rose Finn-Kelcey, *Steam Installation* of 1992, a gigantic metal construction that breathes steam, was first shown at Chisenhale Gallery in London.

Most of the artists whose work is in the gift now live and work in London, although many studied there only after a first degree elsewhere in England, Ireland, Scotland or Wales. Their different histories, which are outlined in the biographical section of this publication, reveal a variety of perspectives and personal strategies for making their presence felt in the art world. This is well demonstrated among the artists who were in *Sensation* – Glenn Brown, Adam Chodzko, Keith Coventry, Paul Finnegan, Mark Francis, John Frankland, Alex Hartley, Abigail Lane, Langlands & Bell, Jonathan Parsons, Hadrian Pigott and Jane Simpson. The mood of the work ranges from aggressive, irreverent and naughty, to seductive, cool and contemplative. It is a tribute to Charles Saatchi that the breadth of his taste has enabled so many kinds of artists to be taken under his wing and promoted as part of YBA culture. Most of these artistic endeavours are essentially critical, and if they appear to be developing traditional forms of figuration, portraiture, landscape and abstraction it is to question and even to undermine them. The press focused perhaps too much on what was spectacular in *Sensation* and paid less attention to the seriousness, and refinement, that is at the heart of much of this work.

The immediacy and appeal of some work in the gift arises from the use of familiar and odd objects that combine a kind of Dadaistic irreverence with an acknowledgement of tendencies in recent American contemporary work such as that of Jeff Koons.[6] These objects are as disparate as Jordan Baseman's doll, Darren Lago's hairdryer, Carina Weidle's balloon, Katharine Dowson's bubbling glass, Abigail Lane's ink pad, Nina Saunders' sprouting chair, John Isaacs' diode recliner, Jonathan Parsons' monochrome flag, Martin Boyce's souvenir placards and Hadrian Pigott's hygienic items. In their altered states they have unexpected power to enchant and repel.

When it comes to portraiture, the intestinal antics of John Greenwood's surrealist painting turn the genre inside out, while Emma Rushton provides only houses and names and no inhabitants. The voyeuristic intrusion of the media lens informs Richard Billingham's powerful family photographs and Chantal Joffe's vivid sketches. Joanna Kirk's outsize pastels reveal her parents larger than life, and Glenn Brown turns the face of a little girl into that of a giant. Claude Heath's portraits are mapped by touch. Siobhán Hapaska is not alone among artists in the gift in making waxwork figures to achieve stunning verisimilitude. Kerry Stewart manages a lighter vein with entrancingly banal fibreglass characters.

The abstract painters Mark Francis, Simon Callery, John Wilkins and Brad Lochore restrict themselves to working in monochrome, or nearly so. Francis seals images of microbiological cell structures into exquisite surfaces. Wilkins' sausage and snowflake motifs are distant reflections of painted marks and famous paintings. Both Callery and Lochore deal with light: Callery as it glances off architecture whose structures he subtly articulates, and Lochore by painting shadow grids of windows which challenge the achievements of the cinema and photography. Nicholas May, by contrast, uses intense colour, floating minerals and pigment in flat glossy surfaces that appear to ripple like glowing planets. The curious figurative paintings of Liz Arnold and Daniel Coombs comment on Modernism.

The works mentioned above are just some of those included in the gift but provide a taste of the variety and quality of work. The entire gift is illustrated in this book, where work by each artist is represented. Readers and researchers may use this catalogue to imagine what an exhibition of the whole gift would be like. In fact, now that it is integrated into the Collection, these works will rarely, if ever, be on view all together.

Following formal acceptance of the donation and its public announcement, galleries were quick to request loans and make their own selection for exhibitions, confining themselves initially entirely to works from the gift. The first work to go out was a costly and difficult project for any venue: John Frankland's golden lift lobby *You Can't Touch This*. Stored as a neat roll of polythene, its installation involves the creation of an immaculate wood framework on which the polythene is heated and stretched, a process involving two weeks' work in collaboration with the artist. The result, at Arnolfini in Bristol, was glorious, an immediate vindication of the gift if any were needed. The Mappin Art Gallery in Sheffield also mounted an exhibition of twenty-three loans. The Mead Gallery at the University of Warwick chose to combine Saatchi works with other recent Arts Council Collection purchases. Other displays from the gift are now showing at the Art Institute in Bournemouth, the Towner Art Gallery in Eastbourne, and Peterborough Museum and Art Gallery. Works are available individually as well as in cluster loans so that they are fully absorbed into the Collection and its activities.

Time alone will ultimately test how enduring recent British artistic activity, as represented in this generous donation, will be. Throughout its life the Arts Council Collection has chosen to tread a speculative path by supporting the work of young artists. To be entrusted with one hundred works of art by such a conspicuous and perceptive benefactor endorses and publicizes the Collection's aims and activities. It also, most importantly, enhances the Collection in a manner that all the more effectively reflects the heightened temperature of British art in the 1990s.

Isobel Johnstone, Curator, Arts Council Collection
February 2000

raising the temperature 100°

Notes

1. The first exhibitions at the Saatchi Gallery were *Donald Judd, Brice Marden, Cy Twombly, Andy Warhol* (March–October 1985), *Carl Andre, John Chamberlain, Dan Flavin, Sol Lewitt, Robert Ryman, Frank Stella* (December 1985–July 1986) and *Anselm Kiefer, Richard Serra* (September 1986–July 1987), followed in 1988 by the first of two shows of *New York Art Now*. Other artists shown between 1988 and 1992 include Philip Guston, Sigmar Polke, Jennifer Bartlett, Erich Fischl, Bruce Nauman, Leon Kossoff, Bill Woodrow, Frank Auerbach, Lucian Freud, Richard Deacon and Cindy Sherman.

2. Formerly Saatchi & Saatchi, a world-class advertising agency.

3. Richard Shone, 'From *Freeze* to *House*: 1988–94' in *Sensation: Young British Artists from the Saatchi Collection*, Royal Academy of Arts, London, 18 September–28 December 1997, p. 14.

4. The Saatchi Gallery series of exhibitions devoted to younger British artists were as follows: *Young British Artists I* (March–October 1992): John Greenwood, Damien Hirst, Alex Landrum, Langlands & Bell, Rachel Whiteread; *Young British Artists II* (February–July 1993): Rose Finn-Kelcey, Sarah Lucas, Marc Quinn, Mark Wallinger; *Young British Artists III* (February–July 1994): Simon Callery, Simon English, Jenny Saville; *Young British Artists IV* (April–June 1995): John Frankland, Marcus Harvey, Brad Lochore, Marcus Taylor, Gavin Turk; *Young British Artists V* (September–December 1995): Glenn Brown, Keith Coventry, Hadrian Pigott, Kerry Stewart; *Young British Artists VI* (September–December 1996): Jordan Baseman, Daniel Coombs, Claude Heath, John Isaacs, Nina Saunders.

5. The Collection already owned prints by Darren Almond, Dinos and Jake Chapman, Mat Collishaw, Sarah Lucas, Sam Taylor-Wood and Mark Quinn, who were also in *Sensation*.

6. *New York Art Now (Part 1)* (September 1987–January 1988): Ashley Bickerton, Ross Bleckner, Robert Gober, Peter Halley, Jeff Koons, Tim Rollins & K.O.S., Haim Steinbach, Philip Taaffe, Meyer Vaisman; *New York Art Now (Part 2)* (February–April 1988): Ashley Bickerton, Carroll Dunham, Robert Gober, Pater Halley, Tishan Hsu, Jon Kessler, Jeff Koons, Allan McCollum, Peter Schuyff, Doug & Mike Starn; *Young Americans* (January–May 1996): Janine Antoni, Gregory Green, Jacqueline Humphries, Sean Landers, Charles Long, Tony Oursler, Richard Prince, Charles Ray, Kiki Smith; *Young Americans 2 (Part One)* (April–July 1998): Ashley Bickerton, Carroll Dunham, David Salle, Jessica Stockholder, Terry Winters; *Young Americans 2 (Part Two)* (September–November 1998): Michael Ashkin, John Currin, Tom Friedman, Martin Kersels, Clay Ketter, Robin Lowe, Josiah McElheny, Sarah Morris, Laura Owens, Elizabeth Peyton, Monique Prieto, Brian Tolle, Sue Williams, Lisa Yuskavage.

the saatchi gift

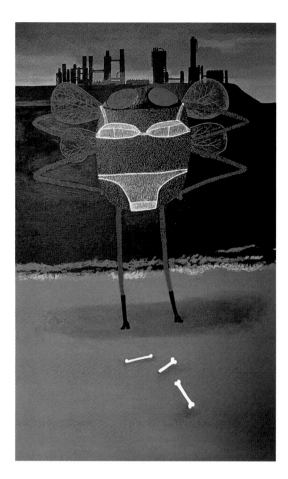

Uncovered shows Secret Agent Greenfly – an eco-detective posing as a beach holiday-maker. My ongoing concern is with the extraordinary human intervention into the so-called 'natural' world – playing with fragile eco-systems. In the painting the plants and animals mutate and adopt human habits and addictions to survive.

I am interested in the creaturely aspects of being a human being. The painting shows a parallel world to the 'real' world – a fantasy place – dreams, fantasies and fictions are part of our experience of the world. *Felicity* celebrates being alive and animal.

Uncovered
1995
Acrylic on canvas
122 x 76 cm

Felicity
1996
Acrylic on canvas
73 x 75 cm

liz arnold

CAPTORS MURDER ISRAELI SOLDIER

CAPTORS MURDER ISRAELI SOLDIER

CAPTORS MURDER IS RAELI SOLDIER

CAPTORS MURDER IS RAELIS OLDIER

CAPTORS MURDERS RAFLIS A LDER

XJS MURDER WIFE NAMED

XJS MURDER WIFE NAMED

XJS MURDER WIFE NAMED

Stress Fracture
1994
Acrylic on canvas
157.5 x 174 cm

From a large database of front page headlines from the *London Evening Standard*, I chose two to be paired together to introduce an element of semantic noise into seemingly simple linguistic statements. The two headlines were then fed into a computer graphics programme and 'morphed' together.

alan ball

I use human hair because it is an extension of our bodies and directly refers to our animalness. It also refers to our efforts to control, disguise and deny the inherent animal aspects of ourselves.

Boy shows the torso of a man's shirt with a boy's shirt-sleeves.

Pretty Baby
1994
Cotton, leather,
plastic, hair
48 x 14 x 6 cm

Boy
1995
Cotton and metal
103 x 67 x 2.5 cm

jordan baseman

**I have to love you but
I don't have to like you**
1996
Human hair attached
to wall
Variable dimensions

I wanted the work to refer to relationships but to be short-lived, like love
sometimes is.

It is certainly not my intention to shock, to offend, to sensationalize, be political
or whatever. Only to make work that is as spiritually meaningful as I can make it.
Whatever the medium.

Untitled (RAL 47)
1995
SFA4 colour photograph
on aluminium
120 x 80 cm

richard billingham

Solids
1990
Dyed wood veneer
on plywood
5 parts, each
12 x 12 x 11.2 cm
(overall length: 439 cm)

My work has always been concerned with the representation of the everyday, with what Jasper Johns has called 'things we see, but never look at'.

terence bond

Protest has become an antiquated notion that I associate with distant places and past decades. It is now inexorably linked with the music and fashion of its time. These words in these configurations are simply unfashionable. We couldn't say them now even if we had to.

Souvenir Placards (Standard Edition)
1993
Wood, emulsion and gloss paint
Variable dimensions

martin boyce

Exercise One
1995
5 c-type colour prints
Each 192 x 139 cm

The original painting was found in a pile of rubbish near London Bridge. I was interested in the power and change of personality that the re-presenting of this painting gave the girl. Her innocence and charming smile become dominating as if she were a dictator.

glenn brown

Think of the frowning Pietà as it contemplates its own creation. Isolated from the expressive pose of the body in its entirety the gesture of the hand is humbled and becomes ambiguous: hanging in rest, weighing something up, unenthusiastically offering.

Untitled (hand)
1994
Silicone, plaster
55 x 32 x 22 cm

phil brown

Borough and Trinity
1993
Oil and oil pastel
on canvas
259.5 x 366 cm

During the late 1980s and early 1990s life in the East End of London was dominated by the redevelopment of the docklands. *Borough and Trinity* was made in response to this. Its linear structure is an articulation of the grammar of architecture under construction. The colour and tonality of the painting communicate the luminous character of the light of an aqueous urban environment.

simon callery

My work searches for other possibilities . . . *Secretors* are leakages into the margins of public space, signalling an aberration: communicating something that shouldn't be there: a glitch or flaw in an existing structure. They ooze out a surplus: appearing simultaneously 'too much' and 'too little'.

2101 Km/Hr (Secretor)
1993
Manifestation juice, lead crystal, plastic, acrylic, acetate
34 x 12 x 3 cm

9468 Km/Hr (Secretor)
1993
Manifestation juice, lead crystal, plastic, acrylic, acetate
34 x 12 x 3 cm

adam chodzko

9605 Km/Hr
(Secretor)
1993
Manifestation juice,
lead crystal, plastic,
acrylic, acetate
34 x 12 x 3 cm

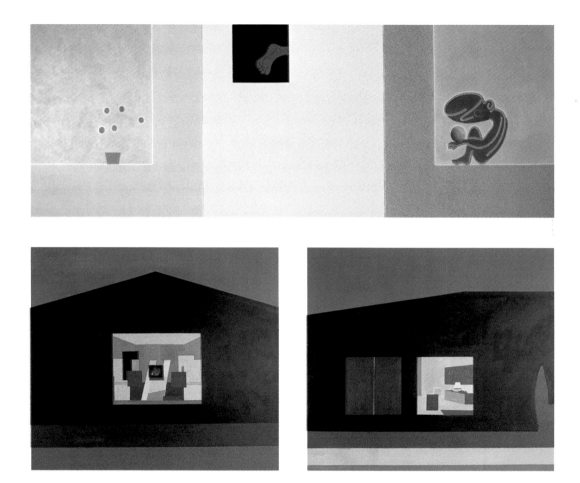

The figure on the right is God, Man is in the middle disappearing down a hole, and on the left is a diagram of the universe in the form of a pot plant.

I was interested in painting the interior almost like a constructivist or cubist painting.

The Creation of the World
1995
Acrylic on canvas
3 parts, each 210 x 210 cm

Night Bungalow I
1995
Acrylic on canvas
213.3 x 243.8 cm

Night Bungalow II
1996
Acrylic on canvas
213.3 x 243.8 cm

daniel coombs

**White Abstract
(Ullein Reviesky, the
last Deb)**
1994
Oil on canvas, wood,
gesso, glass
74.9 x 59.7 x 5.7 cm

White is the colour of international modernism. I wanted to juxtapose this idea against images of privilege, spectacle and tradition, such as changing the guard and gentlemen's clubs. The paintings look like fossils. The institutions are fossilized. All the colour has been drained from the spectacle. Which one is the survivor: modernism or traditionalism?

keith coventry

Three metronomes beating time, one quickly, one slowly and one neither quickly nor slowly.

Work No. 123
1995
Plastic, metal
Diameter: 9.3 cm
Height: 4.6 cm

martin creed

**Untitled 3mm Blue-
November 1995**
1995
Gloss paint, satinwood
on canvas
99.5 x 208.8 cm

I was investigating ways through which I could produce an expressive final image, whilst keeping the number of decisions needed to make each piece to a minimum. The success or failure of the paintings relied on the placement of certain 'accidents' where the final layer of rolled gloss paint bled under its three millimetre mask.

peter davis

I became attracted by close-up photographs of food as they often appeared on supermarket product labels . . . an infinite sea of cornflakes . . . I suppose I was looking for a way to reinvest the city with a sense of the unknown – to reclaim it as the territory of the imagination.

The Lost City
1985
Oil on canvas
53.4 x 71 cm

jeffrey dennis

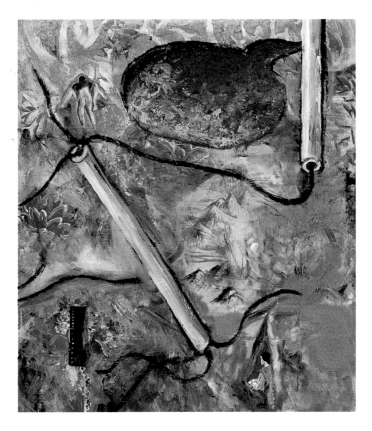

**A Spy in the House
of Frank**
1985
Oil and charcoal on canvas
114.3 x 99 cm

Strange Fruit
1985
Oil and charcoal on canvas
91.5 x 78.7 cm

'Speech' or 'thought' bubbles often appear in my paintings of the time; not so much a graphic sign as a thick encroaching 'cloud' of unbidden thoughts.

Strange Fruit takes as its starting point a William Morris wallpaper design called *Pomegranate*. I was investigating whether pattern could be a sounding-board for the imagination, and a mirror of anxieties.

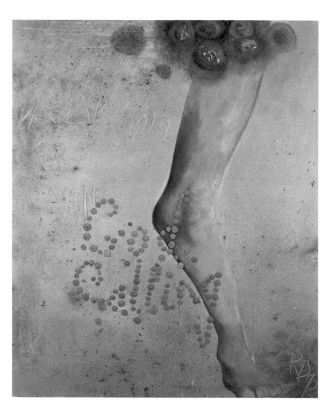

The paintings *Egg Bag* and *Venereal Daze* drew upon the traces and representations that are conjured up by specific disassociated and abject states of being, including Multiple Personality Syndrome, Demonic Possession, Alien Abduction, Stigmata and other hysterical and alienated narratives.

Egg Bag
1991
Oil, dust, silicon and latex prosthetic on canvas
213.5 x 183 cm

Venereal Daze
1992
Oil, dust, silicon and latex prosthetic on canvas
213.5 x 183 cm

rod dickinson

Bubbling Glass
1990
Glass, water, wax, iron,
air pump, plastic tubing
94 x 152.5 x 96.5 cm

Silicon Teats
1992
Silicon, glass, water, wood
83.5 x 98 cm x 54.3 cm

The sound of the water bubbling in the glass echoes the sounds from within the tummy, the digestive juices. It was the start of my exploration into the hidden side of life.

The pink anatomical shadows cast on to the table by the glass forms remind you of X-rays and Ultrasound scans that illuminate the hidden world within us that, without technical innovation, would remain invisible to our eyes.

katharine dowson

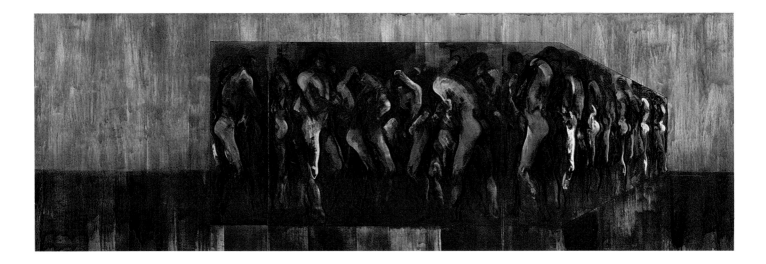

The work sets up a parallel between the gameplay of drawing and the choreography
of performance, adapting the silent 'movie' of the gay cruising bar to become a site
in which to explore the machinations of memory, incident and desire.

Box II (large)
1993
Oil on canvas
3 parts totalling 200 x
600 cm

simon english

'I was once asked at art college to write an essay on how it all began'
1995
Feather, quills, cotton, plasticine
180 x 60 x 60 cm

This work represents a translation of my first 'sculptural solution', a plasticine phallus I made when I was four. This object helped me locate how art began for me and consequently where its significance lay for me.

rachel evans

It is as if an old religious painting has been swamped by its own gold sky leaving only a fragment of the original image remaining. The fragments refer to the point of most intimate physical contact between the Mother and the Child . . . In Early Renaissance paintings gold, because it does not tarnish, symbolized divine light; in my paintings it becomes a concealing device.

The Greek Madonna
1993
Oil and gold leaf on panel
60 x 44 cm

mark fairnington

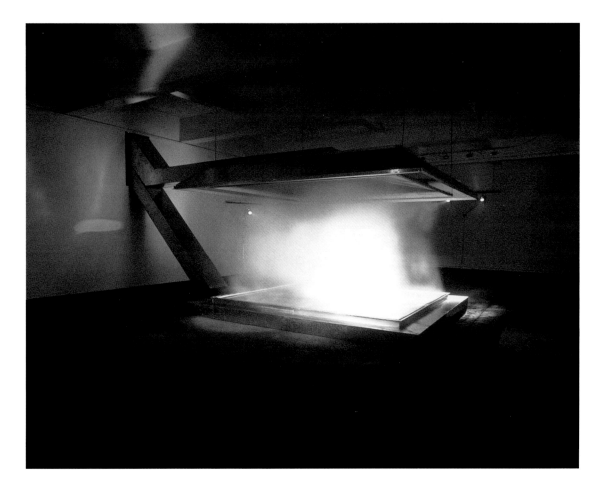

Steam Installation
1992
Steel, water, steam
350 x 350 x 200 cm

This splendid sculpture arouses contrasting associations: rising through majestic, billowing clouds in an aircraft, on the one hand, and luxuriating in the sweaty lassitude of a sauna, on the other.

Sarah Kent, *Young British Artists II*, exhibition catalogue, The Saatchi Gallery, London, 1993

rose finn-kelcey

Car No. 2 shows the dramatic relationship between painting (illusion) and photography (reality). If you believe this exotic car is real, its seamless skin suggests an unknown technology went to make it.

Spuriosis I and *II* are supposed to be hallucinations captured by the camera. Really they are made by placing a real blob of paint on to a transparency of an empty road and then re-photographing the result. The ghostly object appears to hover in space on collision course with the car.

Car No. 2
1995
R-type photographic print
72 x 72 cm

paul finnegan

Spuriosis I
1995
R-type photographic print
72 x 105 cm

Spuriosis II
1995
R-type photographic print
72 x 105 cm

These paintings refer to the positive and negative aspects of photographic
reproduction. I was inspired by looking at biological electron micrographs of
'reproduction' in animal, human and plant forms. The found images were used
purely as a starting point from which I could mutate and manipulate, then use in a
predominately abstract language.

Positive
1992
Oil on canvas
76 x 76 cm

mark francis

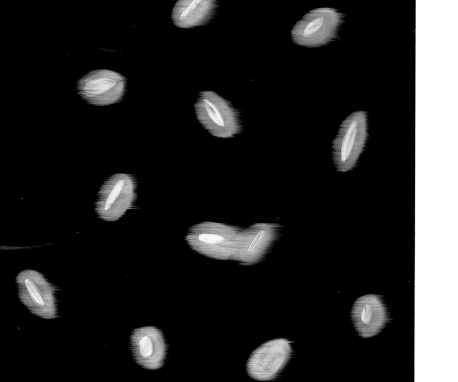

Untitled (Negative 2)
1992
Oil on canvas
107 x 91.5 cm

I had been studying flat surfaces for years, and making lots of them in fairly conventional ways using wood, sand/cement render and plaster. My work came to combine architectural flatness with my favourite aspects of painting. And sculpture.

You Can't Touch This
1992-93
Laminated polythene, wood
Variable dimensions
Photograph taken at Arnolfini, Bristol, 1999

john frankland

Talking Dead
1994
Painted plaster, synthetic
and human hair, resin,
eyes, clothing, refuse
sack, gaffer tape, trunk
91 x 96 x 51 cm

The sculpture *Talking Dead* emerged from an interest in the uncanny and imaginary and altered states of mind. The practice of ventriloquism is often used to symbolize fragmented personalities, where the dummy is endowed with a personality and life of its own. *Talking Dead* combines representations of the generic ventriloquist's dummy and a characteristic method of disposing of victim's bodies practised by murderers.

alison gill

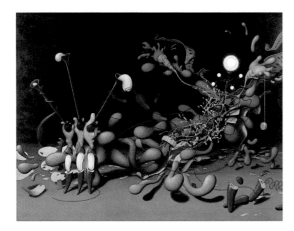

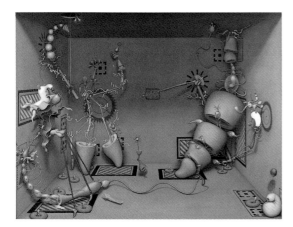

I wanted to create shapes that give form to the yearnings and sensations that flow through us, yet which obey no anatomical logic and can't be captured by external viewing of our physiognomy.

Enjoy Yourself
1991
Oil on canvas
138 x 183 cm

How Many Doughnuts Have You Collected?
1992
Oil on canvas
138 x 183 cm

john greenwood

Mount Hood   *Ray Atkeson*

Airline No. 2
1990
Black and white
photograph, LEDs
117 x 178 cm

This image is re-photographed from a book called *Our Beautiful Land* which is a book of images of the American landscape taken just after the Second World War . . . a heavily romanticized publication. The red LED lights scattered across the surface of the image represent airports across different parts of the globe, so they are really points of arrival or departure. I was interested in these two senses of place coming together, colliding perhaps.

graham gussin

Saint Christopher, the physical manifestation of an idea no longer officially sanctioned, sits with his legs worn down to stumps by years of dedication to his role . . . I wanted to reinstate Saint Christopher as an icon of hope for all people who have been used and discredited by orthodox power structures beyond their control.

Saint Christopher
1995
Wax, hair, cotton, oil paint
90 x 50 x 70 cm

siobhán hapaska

Untitled (Miro)
1992
Satin acid-etched glass,
MDF, photograph
60 x 85 x 11 cm

This is one of only a few works whose subject matter (the empty Modernist gallery)
was taken from a real space. I was working as a gallery photographer for several
galleries, and became interested in the power of the installation shot as the primary
method of dissemination of the artwork.

alex hartley

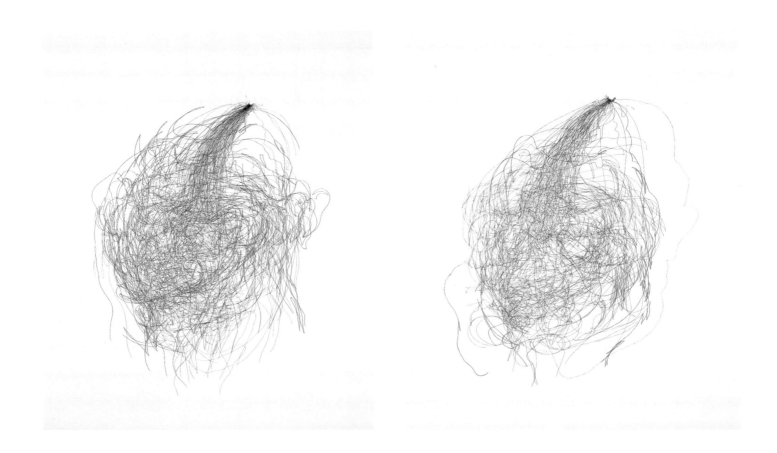

These paintings are based on drawings made blindfold using the sense of touch, feeling the plaster cast of the face with my left hand and simultaneously drawing what I feel with the other.

Tender Ground No. 1
Tender Ground No. 2
Tender Ground No. 3
Tender Ground No. 4
1996
Chalk, oil-based paint and
acrylic on canvas
Each 376 x 315 cm

claude heath

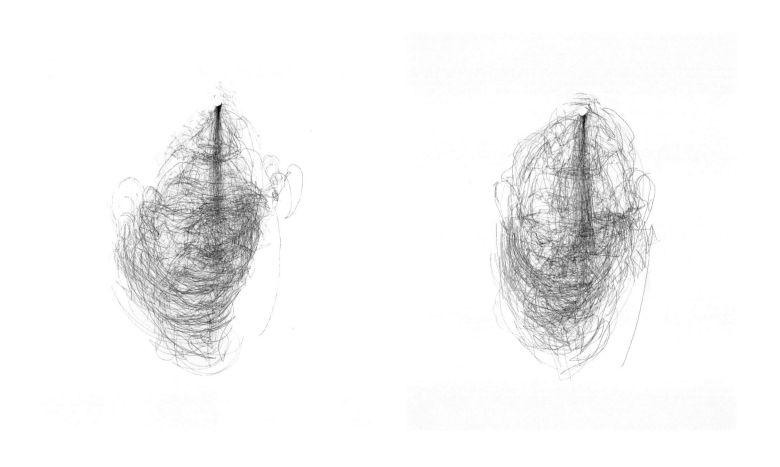

The table was the existing gallery leaflet and information table. The gallery owner particularly disliked the 'fancy elm' grain in the wood. I exaggerated the wood grain by mirroring the elaborate shapes on to the wall using electrical cable.

Wall I
1993
Wood, plastic, metal
75.5 x 152.5 x 55.7 cm

nicky hirst

Aurora 13
1995-96
Oil on reverse of
furnishing fabric
183 x 130 cm

Commercially available furnishing fabric with a flower design is turned over and stretched like canvas. The print in the material shows through faintly from the back to the front. A large area of the pattern/flowers is re-painted in brown and white paint, using the same type of gestural marks that exist in the design. This series became a way of making a painting without overt personal expression.

louise hopkins

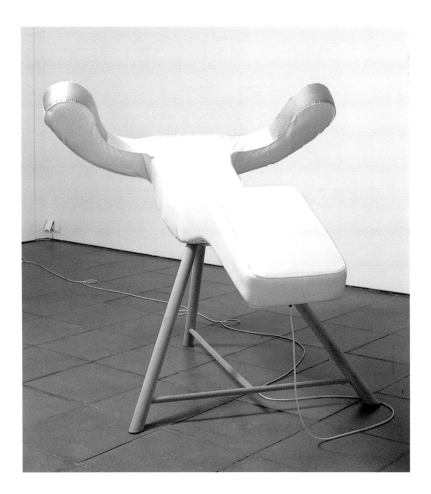

The separation between disciplines and within disciplines is a crucial aspect of Western thought. Individual pursuits have their own momentum; it's impossible to have an overview, a sense of responsibility. We're obsessed with the idea of progress.

Untitled (The Beast With a Million Eyes)
1995
Vinyl, speakers, flex, wood
120 x 90 x 110 cm

john isaacs

Untitled (Monkey)
1995
Wax, hair, glass,
metal, plastic
50 x 40 x 30 cm

This is a group of paintings I made from images of children in mail-order catalogues.
I wanted to give back to the children a sense of their individuality.

Untitled
1995-96
6 paintings, all oil on board
Each 28 x 21.5 cm

chantal joffe

Margaret and *Michael* are my parents. Since 1994 the subject matter of my work has always concentrated on portraits of people close to me. They are larger than life, statuesque even, each having their own canvas to emphasize their individuality.

Margaret
1994
Pastel on paper
241 x 149 cm

Michael
1994
Pastel on paper
241 x 149 cm

joanna kirk

Ferrari Snow
1996
Plastic, paint
16 x 26 x 9 cm

This is Not a Pipe
1996
Briar wood, plastic, metal
13.5 x 25 x 6 cm

Ferrari Snow: My detergent is faster than yours. This elongated 'Fairy Snow' detergent bottle adopts the sculptural language of the supercar.

This is Not a Pipe: In 1923 Le Corbusier held up an image of a pipe as an operative example of purity. Magritte's spectacular riposte was his debased drawing. Mine is an impure functionalism.

darren lago

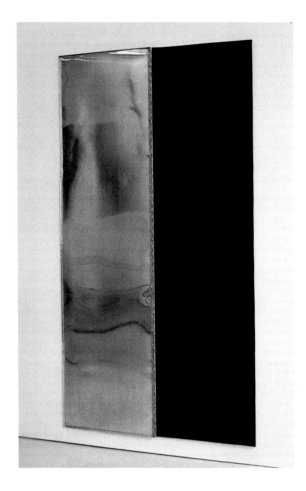

[*Ink Pad I*] contains a felt pad impregnated with black ink to resemble a large abstract painting... Ink pads are normally the source rather than the site of mark making, objects to be used rather than looked at: potential rather than product... they seem to speak in the future tense.

House and Occupants I and *II* explore the allied issues of categorization and status... Lane's photographs of the gallery further complicate the issue by making no distinction between visitors, guards, exhibits and their reflections.

Sarah Kent, *Shark Infested Waters*, Zwemmer, London, 1994

Ink Pad I
1991
Aluminium, MDF, cotton-
covered felt, black ink
168 x 92 x 1.5 cm

abigail lane

House and Occupants I
1991
Photograph, glass
49.5 x 39 x 1.5 cm

House and Occupants II
1991
Photograph, glass
49.5 x 39 x 1.5 cm

These works are from a series of ten works based on the plans of the headquarters buildings of international banks and business conglomerates in Germany – chosen because they embody the 'logocentric' corporate culture and design strategies employed by these corporations.

D.G. Bank, Frankfurt
1990
Wood, paint, lacquer, glass
90 x 90 x 15 cm

langlands & bell

Rank Xerox, Düsseldorf
1990
Wood, paint, lacquer, glass
90 x 90 x 15 cm

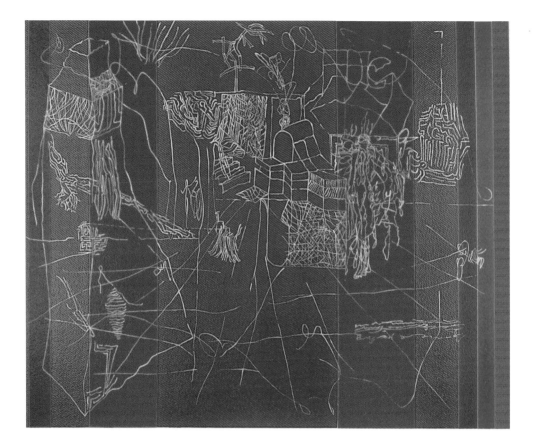

Paint is applied to the canvas with a roller, building up a uniformly textured, hard-edged impersonal ground. Delicate, idiosyncratic and intimate linear marks are then painted on to this surface. In essence, the ground and the linear marks on top are poles apart. When they come together they form an extraordinary relationship . . .

Slowburn Escort
1992
Day-glo and interference
acrylic on canvas
171 x 215 cm

david leapman

Pilot Schemer
1992
Acrylic and interference
acrylic on canvas
166 x 216 cm

In the long line of pictures that are made rather than taken, this one closes the gap between habits of looking and a casual encounter. The picture as object slows down consumption, it lingers and resists narrative. It begs no special attention and reveals nothing at first sight.

Strip Light
1991
Black and white
transparency,
painted wooden box,
fluorescent light
30 x 167 x 20 cm

marysia lewandowska

Shadow No. 52
1994
Oil on canvas
290 x 610 cm

This painting is proportioned at the scale of a cinema screen. As 'screen' the window motif casts a shadow of itself as if from a giant skylight. The window shadows are cast across this empty screen from two impossible angles recalling two possible moments of cast light. But these shadows have no actual origin as they are generated by a computer.

brad lochore

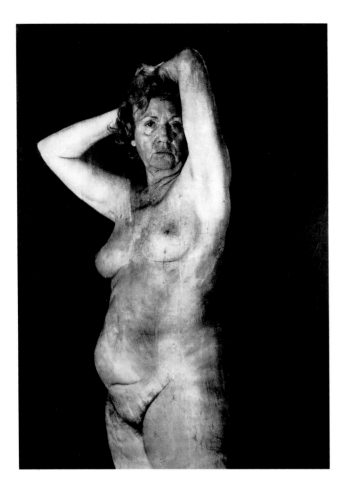

The very fact of working with my mother has direct implications on the precise question of voyeurism that is central to the work . . . The nature of the worked surface makes reference to the texture of skin and relates to the building up of our physical boundary through multiple layers of tissue.

Mrs Manchot, Arms over Head
1996
Silver gelatin and mixed media on canvas
193 x 140 cm

melanie manchot

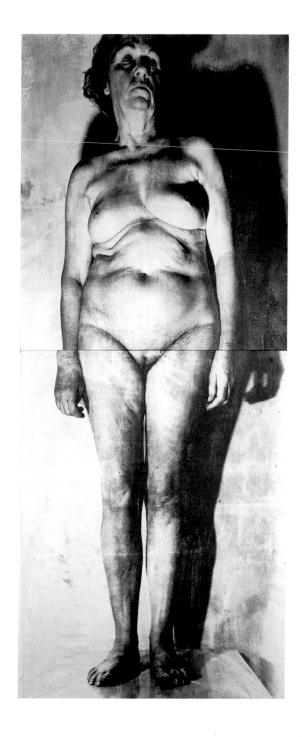

**Mrs Manchot Stands
Tall (diptych)**
1996
Silver gelatin and mixed
media on canvas
260 x 110 cm

Painting is an act of will pitted against the physical. It is a desire with many objects. It is never an object.

Liminal Ellipse (orange)
1996
Acrylic, silicone and
metallic powder on canvas
213.5 x 320 cm

nicholas may

Armour Rien
1996
Oil on canvas
218 x 279 cm

Armour Jamais
1996
Oil on canvas
218 x 218 cm

These images were defiantly vulnerable, hysterical, chauvinist and certainly media-derived. They are stranded in an awareness of being haunted and crippled by the process of reproduction and narcissistic consumption of their image.

ian mclean

What interested me about these snapshots – taken by family and friends – was the excess of detail in the backgrounds – they were microcosms of superfluous information... This type of photography is rarely constructed or composed beyond a kind of record of a person, so by seamlessly removing the figure the image seems hopelessly awkward, irresolvable, haunted. What interested me about this activity was the slippage from the personal realm to the generic materiality that surrounds our lives.

Untitled
1994
15 dye-sublimation photographic prints
8.9x8.5cm, 8.9x8.9cm,
9x8.9cm, 14.1x8.9cm,
8.9x8.9cm, 11x7.8cm,
11.5x8.9cm, 9x8.9cm,
8.5x13cm, 9x8.9cm,
8.7x8.7cm, 10.7x8.8cm,
8.8x8.8cm, 8.8x8.8cm,
8.1x7.8cm

stephen murphy

Stolen Sunsets
1996
Steel, glass, fibreglass,
enamel, dye, acrylic,
water, salt, varnish
180 x 65 x 45 cm

The placement of the tiny cross on the main peak in *Stolen Sunsets* is crucial to the work as it shifts the whole scene into a subjective reading or what we call Romanticism – that is about man's relationship to nature and the sublime.

mariele neudecker

Blind Faith draws on my experience of working in an office, the artist's workspace and the art display space. It draws on my scientific background in which experience is explained with models and mathematical constructs.

Blind Faith
1992
Mixed media
244 x 244 x 366 cm

renato niemis

Achrome
1994
Polyester, cotton, wood,
rope
457 x 228 cm

The use of the word 'Achrome' is intended to suggest the representation of a coloured object rendered simply without colour. As such, this flag is a picture of the tonal values of the most familiar coloured object I could find, the Union flag.

jonathan parsons

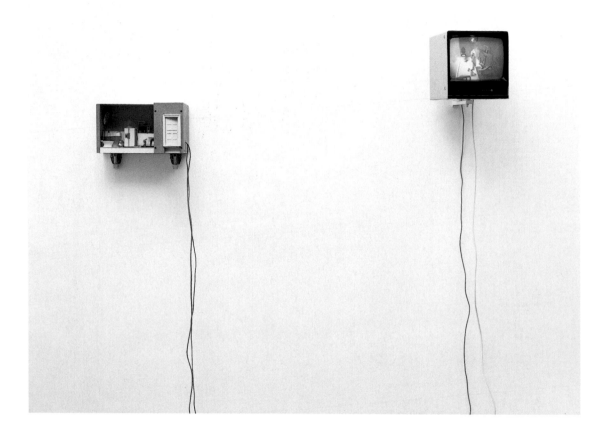

The model depicts a laboratory or even a cell – at the very least a place where an experiment is to be carried out in isolation... From the details/props within the room we can discern that the test is to be made upon a human subject, and we might assume a bio-chemical study will be made over a period of time.

**Meanwhile at the
Marie Curie School of
Organic Chemistry...**
1995
Mixed media
17.4 x 32.5 x 24 cm
and 23 x 22 x 25 cm

gary perkins

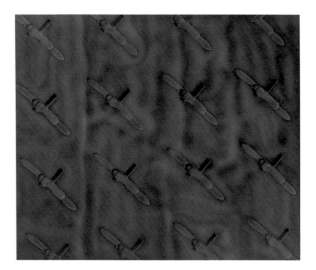

Blank III: The shape is an imagining, a coalescing of form of basin, bar of soap and body.

Fleeting is one of a series of panels depicting the things people carry about their persons – small pointers to social position and identity. The repeated 'empty image' of a knife (the original was a discarded plastic point-of-sale display tray for Swiss army knives) was to indicate sameness in apparent choice available to us across the counter.

Blank III
1995
Pink soap, plastic
shrinkwrap, chromed
plastic
30 x 85 x 45 cm

Fleeting
1995
Fibreglass relief panel
with flocked surface
255 x 300 x 12 cm

hadrian pigott

**Wash 1
(Self-position 1 – London
23rd March 1994)**
1994
White soap, painted plaster
18 parts, each
8 x 13 x 8.5 cm
With thanks to the
Typography Studio at the
Royal College of Art

Wash 1 is a self-portrait. It depicts the body of the artist through the act of washing.

An aftermath scene from a disaster or riot . . . Despite the violent narratives,
I was more concerned with using three or four different blues to model figures
with solidity but without tonal naturalism.

Blue Pietà
1992
Oil on canvas
183 x 183 cm

joanna price

Object of Fun
1995
Oil on canvas
213.4 x 182.9 cm

I'd recently become a dad. This had a massive effect on my work: most of my paintings reflected family life in some way.

james rielly

I need a time machine.

Space
1995
Paint, photographs,
paper, wood, glass,
metal, plastic
Variable dimensions

gary rough

Raphe (Businessmen)
1992
Plasticard, printed brick
and tile paper, perspex,
gravel, paint, M.D.F
114 x 30 x 20 cm

Chris (Businessmen)
1992
Plasticard, printed brick
paper, perspex, paint,
M.D.F
158.7 x 24.3 x 24.3 cm

Detached four bedroom house.	1992	£230,000
	1999	£405,000
Split level two bedroom flat over trading premises.	1992	£72,000
	1999	£195,000

emma rushton

While I was in Denmark, my husband threw away the sofa on which we had fallen in love. I was devastated.

Unfinished Opera
1996
Plastic, fabric, cotton, wood
67 x 57 x 108 cm

nina saunders

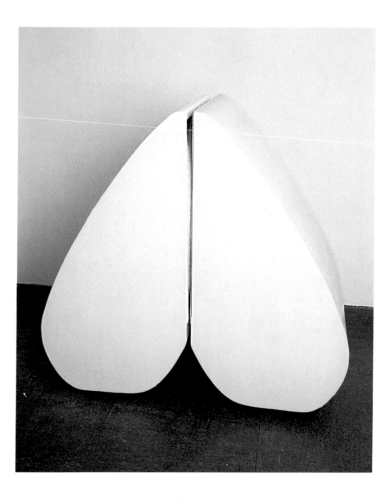

Between
1992
Wood, brass, plastic,
ice, refrigeration units,
castors, steel
127 x 115.5 x 62 cm

It was based on a heart shape, inverted and split in two . . . the idea was to switch it
on and let the build up of ice on each surface slowly fuse together.

jane simpson

Lucy is from Lucy, the earliest proto-human, in the Natural History Museum . . .
I like the figure of Lucy because I think she was found on her own; she is the only
representative.

Untitled (Lucy)
1996
Fibreglass, enamel
152 x 50 x 35 cm

kerry stewart

Untitled (Upright Fridge)
1991
Clear acrylic sheet
124 x 66 x 61 cm

In a sense it was an attempt to trap and solidify the air around it, to blur the distinction between solid and ephemeral, to create an intangible moment between solid and vapour.

marcus taylor

One of the main interests in *Blank and Flat* was the fragile equilibrium between the parts, one depending absolutely on the other . . . to have the air, that is a substance that usually we have around us, malleable and passive, supporting weight and being the very structure of a work was attractive to me . . . it carries with it the potential of a catastrophe.

Blank and Flat
1992
Wax, balloon
46 x 100 x 70 cm

carina weidle

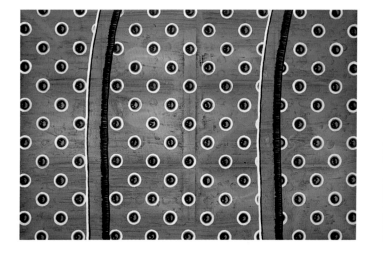

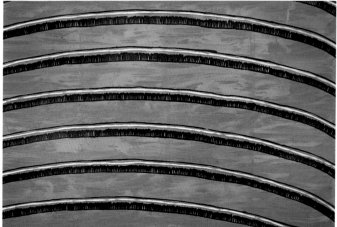

Winterwonderland
1993
Acrylic on canvas
244 x 366 cm

Dancing in the Dark
1993
Acrylic on canvas
244 x 366 cm

Winterwonderland: The movement from art historical origin to these strange worlds might also be compared with the linguistic movement in a game of Chinese Whispers: creativity formed through the formalization of mishearings or bastardized interpretations.

Dancing in the Dark: The sausage shapes were originally an absurd remodelling of the modernist painted mark . . . But since then, the damn things, they get out of control . . .

Martin Herbert, *John Wilkins*, exhibition catalogue, Centro de Arte S João da Madeira, 1998

john wilkins

The whole work is based on contrast: precariousness and fragility against rigidity and strength; hiding and revealing. A lattice panel system is common to both the wall and the greenhouse. The once private, hidden area of an exhibiting space is now on show, exposed.

High Rise
1989
Glass greenhouse, steel beams, 2 insect-o-cutors
244 x 396 x 366 cm

richard wilson

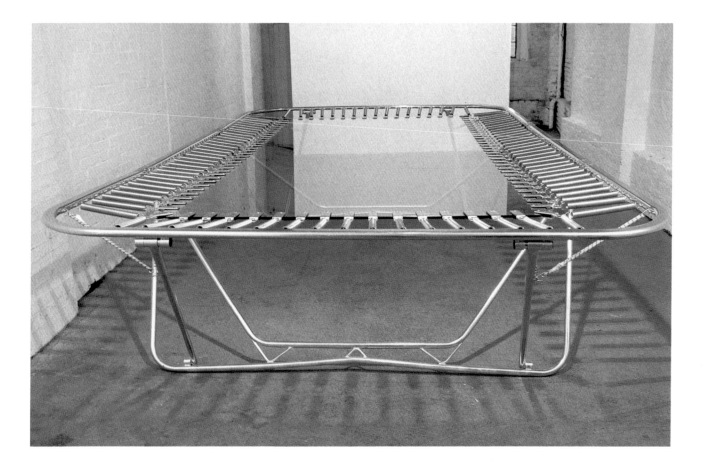

Can't Play, Won't Play
1996
Glass, steel
150 x 291 x 550 cm

The components that a person would use to facilitate different bodily movements have been replaced with glass . . . this makes this physical equipment totally functionless and static.

lucy wood

In using the car as 'canvas' as opposed to just subject matter, I am encouraging the paint to be read as an object, and the text under the images gives the paint a more pragmatic *alter ego*.

**Austin Metro (Red),
Deptford**
1996
Enamel paint on
printed canvas
245 x 366 cm

**Peugeot 205 (Blue),
Bermondsey**
1996
Enamel paint on
printed canvas
243.8 x 365.7 cm

richard woods

**Volkswagen Golf
(Green), Old Kent Road**
1996
Enamel paint on
printed canvas
245 x 366 cm

**BMW 525 as Biological
Experiment (Green)**
1996
Enamel paint on
printed canvas
25.4 x 39.4 cm

biographies

Liz Arnold was born in Perth, Scotland, in 1964. She studied at Middlesex Polytechnic (1987–90) and Goldsmiths College, London (1992–94). Her work has been included in *New Contemporaries*, Tate Gallery Liverpool (1996), *Interesting Painting*, City Racing, London (1997) and *Anxiety*, Collective Gallery, Edinburgh (1999). She has had solo exhibitions at Lotta Hammer, London (1999) and Chicago Project Room (1999). She lives and works in London.

Alan Ball was born in London in 1962. He studied at Goldsmiths College, London (1984-87). His recent exhibitions have included *Parallel Lines*, Golden Arrow House, London (1995), *United in Death*, Cambridge Darkroom Gallery (1998) and *Forest*, Bull and Last, London (1998). He is included in the CD-Rom *On Boredom*, Cambridge Darkroom Gallery (1997). In 1998 he co-curated the inaugural exhibition, *Pretty Vacant*, at Artezium Arts and Media Centre, Luton. He lives and works in London.

Jordan Baseman was born in Philadelphia, USA, in 1960. He studied at the Tyler School of Art, Philadelphia (1979-83) and then moved to London, continuing his studies at Goldsmiths College (1986-88). His solo exhibitions include *The Party and Other Things*, Richard Salmon Gallery, London (1997), *blunt objects*, Galerie Eugen Lendl, Graz (1997) and *More Lies*, Mario Flecha Gallery, Girona (1998). Group exhibitions include *British Art Show 4* (1995) and *Fetishism* (1995), both National Touring Exhibitions from the Hayward Gallery, London, *Pictura Britannica*, British Council tour (1997-98) and *Personal Effects*, Spacex Gallery, Exeter (1998). He has published a screenplay *SHUP* (Bookworks, 1998). He lives and works in London.

Richard Billingham was born in Birmingham in 1970. He graduated from University of Sunderland in 1994 and took part in his first group exhibition, *Who's Looking at the Family?*, at the Barbican Art Gallery, London, in the same year. He was awarded the first Citibank Photography Prize in 1997. He has had solo exhibitions at the National Museum of Film and Photography, Bradford (1996), Anthony Reynolds Gallery, London (1996, 1998), Luhring Augustine, New York (1997), Regen Projects, Los Angeles (1997) and Jennifer Flay, Paris (1998). Photographs from this series have been published in the book *Ray's a Laugh* (Scalo, 1996). He lives and works in Stourbridge.

Terence Bond was born in Epping in 1960. He studied at Wolverhampton Polytechnic (1978-81) and Royal College of Art, London (1984-86). He has been included in the group exhibitions *Wonderful Life*, Lisson Gallery, London (1993), *Ideal Standard Summer Time* and *Postscript*, Lisson Gallery, London (1995) and *Being Human*, Woodlands Gallery, London (1999). He lives and works in London.

Martin Boyce was born in Glasgow in 1967. He studied at Glasgow School of Art (1986-90 and 1995-97). His solo exhibitions include Loggia Gallery, Toronto (1996), Lotta Hammer, London (1999) and Fruitmarket Gallery, Edinburgh (1999). Group exhibitions have included *Live/Life*, Musée d'Art Moderne de la Ville de Paris (1996), *Material Culture*, Hayward Gallery, London (1997), *Nettwerk-Glasgow*, Museet for Samtidskunst, Oslo (1998) and *Anarchitecture*, De Appel Foundation, Amsterdam (1999). He lives and works in Glasgow.

Glenn Brown was born in Northumberland in 1966. He studied at Bath College of Higher Education (1985-88) and Goldsmiths College, London (1990-92). His recent solo exhibitions include Queen's Hall Arts Centre, Hexham (1996), Jerwood Gallery, London (1999) and Patrick Painter, Los Angeles (1999). He was also included in *Belladonna*, Institute of Contemporary Arts, London (1997), *Pure Fantasy*, Oriel Mostyn, Llandudno (1997) and *Examining Pictures*, Whitechapel Art Gallery, London (1999). He curated *It's a Curse, It's a Burden* at The Approach, London, in 1998. He lives and works in London.

Phil Brown was born in Bury, Lancashire, in 1972. He attended Slade School of Art, London (1991-95) and has exhibited in several group shows including *Ideal Standard Summer Time* and *Postscript*, Lisson Gallery, London (1995), *The Hanging Picnic*, Factual Nonsense, London (1995), *Ad Hoc*, London Art Forms (1996) and *Shift*, The Foundry, London (1999). He lives and works in London.

Simon Callery was born in London in 1960. He studied at Cardiff College of Art (1980-83), but did not exhibit his work publicly until 1989 in the *Whitechapel Open*, London. He has had solo exhibitions at Anthony Wilkinson Fine Art, London (1996), Pitt Rivers Museum, Oxford (1997) and *ArtNow*, Tate Gallery, London (1999). He has also participated in many group exhibitions including *John Moores 18*, Walker Art Gallery, Liverpool (1993), where he was a prize-winner, *About Vision*, MOMA, Oxford (1996) and *Quiet Storm*, Kohn Turner Gallery, Los Angeles (1999). He lives and works in London.

Adam Chodzko was born in London in 1965. He studied History of Art at University of Manchester (1985-88) before completing an MA in Fine Art at Goldsmiths College, London (1992-94). He was awarded a British School in Rome Scholarship in 1997. His recent solo exhibitions include Lotta Hammer, London (1996), Northern Centre for Contemporary Art, Sunderland (1998), Ikon Gallery, Birmingham (1999) and Galleria Franco Noero, Turin (1999). He was also included in *Brilliant!*, Walker Art Center, Minneapolis (1995), *At One Remove*, Henry Moore Institute, Leeds (1997) and *Sleuth*, Ffotogallery, Cardiff (1999). He lives and works in London.

biographies

Daniel Coombs was born in London in 1971. He studied at Ruskin School of Drawing, Oxford (1989-92) and Royal College of Art, London (1992-94), before becoming a Rome Scholar in Painting at the British School in Rome (1994-95). He had a solo exhibition at The Approach, London (1999), and participated in *Paradigms of Oneirology*, One in the Other, London (1998) and *6 min 3 sec* in Tullkammaren, Sweden (1999). He lives and works in London.

Keith Coventry was born in Burnley, Lancashire, in 1958. He studied at Brighton Polytechnic (1978-81) and Chelsea School of Art, London (1981-82). His solo exhibitions include Karsten Schubert, London (1994), Spacex Gallery, Exeter (1997), The Showroom, London (1997), Frahm Gallery, Copenhagen (1998) and Richard Salmon Gallery, London (1998). He has exhibited in many group shows, including *From Here*, Waddington Galleries and Karsten Schubert, London (1995), *Primary Paint*, Museum of Modern Art, San Diego (1997) and *John Moores 21*, Walker Art Gallery, Liverpool (1999). He lives and works in London.

Martin Creed was born in Wakefield in 1968. He studied at Slade School of Art, London (1986-90). He has had solo exhibitions at the British School in Rome (1997), Cabinet Gallery, London (1999) and Southampton City Art Gallery (2000). He has also participated in many group shows, including *Sarah Staton's Supastore Boutique*, Laure Genillard Gallery, London (1994), *Live/Life*, Musée d'Art Moderne de la Ville de Paris (1996) and *everyday*, Sydney Biennale (1998). He lives and works in London.

Peter Davis was born in Sutton, Surrey, in 1972. He studied at Goldsmiths College, London (1990-93). Since then he has had solo shows at Karsten Schubert, London (1994), Slewe Galerie, Amsterdam (1997, 2000), Valentina Moncada, Rome (1999) and Asprey Jacques, London (1999). He has exhibited in many group exhibitions including *From Here*, Waddington Galleries, London and Karsten Schubert, London (1995), *Real Art, A New Modernism*, Southampton City Art Gallery, Stedelijk Museum, Aalst, and Leeds City Art Gallery (1995-96) and Anderson O'Day Gallery, London (1997). He lives and works in Cambridge.

Jeffrey Dennis was born in Colchester in 1958. He studied at Slade School of Art, London (1976-80). His solo exhibitions include Whitechapel Art Gallery, London (1986), Orchard Gallery, Derry (1993), Anderson O'Day Gallery, London (1994) and Chelsea School of Art, London (1999), as well as regular showings at Salvatore Ala Gallery, New York. Recent group exhibitions include *A Cloudburst of Material Possessions*, Towner Art Gallery, Eastbourne, and tour (1997-98), *John Moores 20*, Walker Art Gallery, Liverpool (1997) and *Secret Victorians*, a National Touring Exhibition from the Hayward Gallery, London (1998-2000). He lives and works in London.

Rod Dickinson was born in Southampton in 1965. He studied at Kingston Polytechnic (1986-89). He has participated in many group exhibitions, including *Lovecraft*, Centre for Contemporary Art, Glasgow (1997), *Are We Touched?*, Huntington Beach Art Center, California (1997), *Martin*, Commercial Gallery, London (1997), Waygood Gallery, Newcastle upon Tyne, and Catalyst Arts, Belfast (1998). Solo exhibitions include Cabinet Gallery, London (1992, 1995) and Camerawork, London (1998). His most recent one-person exhibition was at Forum im Dominikanerkloster, Stadtakademie, Frankfurt (1999). He lives and works in London.

Katharine Dowson was born in London in 1962. She studied at Camberwell School of Art, London (1985-88) and Royal College of Art, London (1989-92). Her solo shows include *Growth*, Mayor Gallery, London (1995) and *Myriad*, Whitworth Art Gallery, Manchester (1998). Group exhibitions include *Light*, Richard Salmon Gallery, London (1997) and *Project 8*, Total Museum of Contemporary Art, Seoul (1998). Her work will also be included in the forthcoming *Know Thyself*, Hayward Gallery, London (2000). She lives and works in Northumberland.

Simon English was born in West Berlin in 1959. He studied at Bournemouth College of Art (1977-78) and Central School of Art and Design, London (1978-81). He has worked as a set and costume designer for TARA Arts and also for *Drawing Out Loud*, Chisenhale Dance Space, London (1999). Recent solo exhibitions include *Double and Twist*, Laurent Delaye Gallery, London (1998) and Project Room, Milch, London (1998). Group shows include *Body Double*, Winston Wächter Fine Art, New York (1998), *Il luogo degli Angeli*, Ex Manufactura Tabaschi, Citta Sant'Angelo (1999) and *Sampling*, Ronald Feldman Fine Arts, New York (1999). He lives and works in London.

Rachel Evans was born in Cardiff in 1965. She studied at Manchester Polytechnic (1985-88) and Royal College of Art, London (1988-90). In 1995 she was awarded the Durham Cathedral Artist-in-Residence for one year. Solo exhibitions have included British Council Window Gallery, Prague (1994), Durham Art Gallery (1996) and Eugen Lendl Gallery, Graz (1999). Group exhibitions include *Bad Girls*, Institute of Contemporary Arts, London, and Centre for Contemporary Art, Glasgow (1993), *High Fidelity*, Kohji Ogura Gallery, Nagoya, Japan (1994), *Picture Stories*, Victoria Miro Gallery, London (1997), *Nitty Gritty*, James van Damme Gallery, Brussels (1997) and *Your Place or Mine*, Elga Wimmer, New York (1998). She lives and works in London.

biographies

Mark Fairnington was born in Gateshead in 1957. He studied at St Martin's School of Art, London (1976-80) and Goldsmiths College, London (1987-89). His recent solo exhibitions include Todd Gallery, London (1997) and Gallery Theime and Pohl, Germany (1998). He was included in *Postcards on Photography* at the Cambridge Darkroom Gallery (1998), *Heavier than Air*, Imperial War Museum, London (1998) and *Images of the Flower in 20th Century Art* at Harewood House (1999). In the same year he was awarded the Sargent Fellowship at the British School in Rome. He is currently a tutor in Fine Art at the Ruskin School of Drawing and Fine Art, Oxford University.

Rose Finn-Kelcey was born in Northampton. She studied at Ravensbourne College of Art and Chelsea School of Art, London. She has exhibited widely in the UK and abroad. Solo exhibitions include Ikon Gallery, Birmingham (1994) and Camden Arts Centre, London (1997). Group exhibitions include *Documenta*, Kassel, Germany (1992) and *The British Art Show*, a National Touring Exhibition from the Hayward Gallery, London (1984-85). Her installations include *Steam Installation*, Chisenhale Gallery, London (1992), and *Just Minus* (a refrigerated installation), British School in Rome, Italy (1994). She lives and works in London.

Paul Finnegan was born in London in 1968. He graduated from St Martin's School of Art, London, in 1992. He had solo exhibitions at Entwistle, London (1997) and One in the Other, London (1999). He was included in *Hiatus* at Metro Works (1993) and *Ideal Standard Summer Time* at Lisson Gallery, London (1995). He lives and works in Buckinghamshire.

Mark Francis was born in Newtownards, County Down, Northern Ireland, in 1962. He studied at St Martin's School of Art, London (1980-85) and Chelsea School of Art, London (1985-86). He has had solo exhibitions at Manchester City Art Gallery (1995), Kerlin Gallery, Dublin (1997), Mary Boone Gallery, New York (1997), Maureen Paley Interim Art, London (1994, 1995, 1998) and Milton Keynes Gallery (2000). His recent group exhibitions include *Testing the Water*, Tate Gallery Liverpool (1995), *John Moores 20*, Walker Art Gallery, Liverpool (1997), *Negotiating Small Truths*, College of Fine Arts, University of Texas, Austin (1999) and *Zero Zero Four Four*, PS1, New York, and Albright-Knox Art Gallery, Buffalo (1999). He lives and works in London.

John Frankland was born in Rochdale, Lancashire, in 1961, and studied at Goldsmiths College, London (1980-83). He has had solo exhibitions at Hales Gallery, London (1993, 1994), Matt's Gallery, London (1996), Royal Festival Hall, London (1997) and Project Art Centre, Dublin (1999). Group exhibitions include *British Art Show 4*, a National Touring Exhibition from the Hayward Gallery, London (1995-96), *Belladonna*, Institute of Contemporary Arts, London (1997) and *Pictura Britannica*, British Council tour (1997-98). He lives and works in London.

Alison Gill was born in London in 1966. She studied at Brighton Polytechnic (1985-88) and Royal College of Art, London (1990-92). She was included in *Ideal Standard Summer Time* and *Postscript*, both at Lisson Gallery, London (1995), *Martin*, Commercial Gallery, London (1997), Catalyst Arts, Belfast, and Waygood Gallery, Newcastle upon Tyne (1998) and *Dream Machines*, a National Touring Exhibition from the Hayward Gallery, London (2000). She has had two solo showings at the Sabine Wachters Gallery, Brussels (1996, 1998) and has exhibited with Jacqueline Donachie at Jerwood Gallery, London (1999). Her most recent solo show is Taro Nasu Gallery, Japan (2000). She lives and works in London.

John Greenwood was born in Leeds in 1959. He studied at Cheltenham College of Art (1978-81) and Royal College of Art, London (1988-90). He has had solo exhibitions at Manchester City Art Galleries (1993) and Jason Rhodes Gallery, London (1998). He was also included in *The Discerning Eye*, Mall Galleries, London (1992), *An American Passion*, McLellan Galleries, Glasgow (1995) and *The Modern City in Europe*, Museum of Contemporary Art, Tokyo (1996). He appeared in the *Oil on Canvas* series for BBC television in 1997 and he has designed album covers for Orbital. He lives and works in London.

Graham Gussin was born in London in 1960. He studied at Middlesex Polytechnic (1981-85) and Chelsea School of Art, London (1989-90). He has had solo exhibitions at Chisenhale Gallery, London (1993), Primo Piano, Rome (1993, 1995) and Lotta Hammer, London (1996, 1998). Group exhibitions include *Wonderful Life*, Lisson Gallery, London (1993), *Wall to Wall*, a National Touring Exhibition from the Hayward Gallery, London (1994), *The Meaning of Life*, a video programme at Centre for Contemporary Art, Glasgow, and the Art Node Foundation, Stockholm (1996) and Melbourne International Biennial (1999). He lives and works in London.

Siobhán Hapaska was born in Belfast in 1963. She attended Middlesex Polytechnic, London (1985-88) and Goldsmiths College, London (1990-92). She has had solo exhibitions at Institute of Contemporary Arts, London (1995), Tanya Bonakdar Gallery, New York (1997), Entwistle, London (1997), Oriel, Cardiff (1997) and Saison Art Program Gallery, Tokyo (2000). Group exhibitions include *Documenta X*, Kassel, Germany (1997), *Plastik*, Württembergischer Kunstverein, Stuttgart (1997) and *Speed*, Whitechapel Art Gallery, London (1998). She was the winner of the Glen Dimplex Award at Irish Museum of Modern Art, Dublin, in 1998. She lives and works in London.

biographies

Alex Hartley was born in West Byfleet, Surrey, in 1963. He studied at Camberwell School of Art, London (1983-90) and Royal College of Art, London (1988-90). Recent solo exhibitions include Victoria Miro Gallery, London (1993, 1995, 1997), James van Damme Gallery, Brussels (1997) and Galerie Ulrich Fiedler, Cologne (1998). He has participated in many group exhibitions in the UK and abroad, most recently *Sarajevo 2000*, Museum of Contemporary Art, Sarajevo (1999) and *Il Casa, Il Corpo, Il Curore*, Museum Moderner Kunst Stiftung Ludwig, Vienna (1999). He won the Sculpture at Goodwood Art 2000 Commission Prize. He lives and works in London.

Claude Heath was born in London in 1964. He studied Philosophy at King's College, London (1983-86). He has had solo exhibitions at Hales Gallery, London (1998) and Study Galleries, Leeds City Art Gallery (1999). He has also exhibited in many group exhibitions including *Antechamber*, Whitechapel Art Gallery (1997), *John Moores 20*, Walker Art Gallery, Liverpool (prize-winner, 1997), *Jerwood Painting Prize*, Jerwood Gallery, London (1998) and *Nat West Art Prize*, Lothbury Gallery, London (1999). He lives and works in London.

Nicky Hirst was born in Nottingham in 1963. She studied at Maidstone College of Art (1982-85) and Kent Institute of Art and Design, Canterbury (1993-94). She has had solo exhibitions at the Barbican Foyer Gallery, London (1996), Imperial War Museum, London (1996), Anthony Wilkinson Fine Art, London (1996) and, most recently, a Henry Moore Fellowship Exhibition at Byam Shaw School of Art, London (2000). She has also participated in numerous group exhibitions including *A Cloudburst of Material Possessions*, Towner Art Gallery, Eastbourne, and tour (1997-98) and *Day for Night*, Museum of Installation, London (1999). She lives and works in London.

Louise Hopkins was born in Hertfordshire in 1965. She studied at Newcastle upon Tyne Polytechnic (1985-88) and Glasgow School of Art (1992-94). Her solo exhibitions include Tramway, Glasgow (1996), Raffaella Cortese, Milan (1998) and Andrew Mummery Gallery, London (1999). She was shortlisted for the *Jerwood Painting Prize* in 1997 and has been included in various group exhibitions including *Pictura Britannica*, British Council tour (1997-98), *Nettwerk - Glasgow*, Museet for Samtidskunst, Oslo (1998), *Secret Victorians*, a National Touring Exhibition from the Hayward Gallery, London (1998-99) and *Prime*, Dundee Contemporary Arts (1999). She lives and works in Glasgow.

John Isaacs was born in Lancaster in 1968 and lived as a child in Nigeria. He attended Exeter University (1987-88) where he studied Biology, Dijon Ecole des Beaux Arts (1989) and Slade School of Art, London (1991-93) where he studied Sculpture. His solo exhibitions include *The Matrix of Amnesia*, ArtLab, Imperial College, London (1997), *The incomplete history of unknown discovery*, 20.21 Gallery, Essen (1998) and *The Diary of a Loner*, Chapter Arts Centre, Cardiff (1999). Recent group exhibitions include *Crash*, Camden Arts Centre, London (1997), *Host*, Tramway, Glasgow (1998), *Bad Bad*, Kunsthalle, Baden-Baden (1999) and *A mountain and a valley*, Cubitt Street Gallery, London (1999). He lives and works in London.

Chantal Joffe was born in St Albans in 1969. She studied at Glasgow School of Art (1988-91) and Royal College of Art, London (1992-94). She was awarded an Abbey Scholarship at the British School in Rome in 1998. Her solo exhibitions have included Feigan Gallery, New York (1999) and Il Capricorno, Venice (1999). She has also shown at Victoria Miro Gallery, London, and was included in Saatchi Gallery's *New Neurotic Realism* publication (1998). She lives and works in London.

Joanna Kirk was born in Cheshire in 1963. She studied at Goldsmiths College, London (1981-84). She was awarded joint first prize at the 1987 Artist Award at the Whitechapel Art Gallery, London. Her solo exhibitions include Whitechapel Art Gallery (1988), Todd Gallery, London (1993), Kunsterlerhaus Palais Thurn und Taxis, Bregenz, Austria (1996) and Modern Art Inc., London (1999). She has participated in many group exhibitions including *The British Art Show*, a National Touring Exhibition from the Hayward Gallery, London (1990), *Remaking Reality*, Kettle's Yard, Cambridge (1996) and *The Flower Show*, Harewood House (1999). She lives and works in London.

Darren Lago was born in Walsall in 1965. He studied at Portsmouth Polytechnic (1985-88) and Chelsea School of Art, London (1989-90). He was awarded the Boise Scholarship at Slade School of Art, London, in 1991. His recent solo exhibitions include *Mass* at Walsall Museum and Art Gallery (1993), *Productivism*, Annely Juda Fine Art, London (1996) and 1000 Eventi Gallery, Milan (1999). He was also included in *Fun de Siècle?* at Walsall Museum and Art Gallery (1998). He lives and works in London.

Abigail Lane was born in Penzance in 1967. She studied at Goldsmiths College, London (1986-89). She has had solo exhibitions at Institute of Contemporary Arts, London (1995), Bonnefanten Museum, Maastricht (1996), Victoria Miro Gallery, London (1998), and Museum of Contemporary Art, Chicago (1998). She has also participated in numerous group shows including *Freeze*, Surrey Docks, London (1988), *Ha-Ha*, Killerton House and Spacex Gallery, Exeter (1993), *Some Went Mad, Some Ran Away*, Serpentine Gallery, London (1994), *Material Culture*, Hayward Gallery, London (1997) and *Trance*, Philadelphia Museum of Art (1998). She lives and works in London.

biographies

Ben Langlands was born in London in 1955 and **Nikki Bell** was born in London in 1959. They both studied Fine Art at Middlesex Polytechnic (1977-80) and have been collaborating since 1978. They have had solo exhibitions at Serpentine Gallery, London (1996, plus tour to Bielefeld, Palermo, San Sebastian), the Centre for Contemporary Art, Kitakyushu (1997), TN Probe, Tokyo (1998) and *Opening/Capture*, Center for British Art at Yale (1999). They have also participated in *Architecture as Metaphor*, Museum of Modern Art, New York (1997), 47th Venice Biennale (1997), *Artranspennine98*, Henry Moore Institute, Leeds (1998) and *Graphic! British Art Now*, Center for British Art at Yale (1999). They live and work in London.

David Leapman was born in London in 1959. He attended St Martin's School of Art, London (1977-78) and Goldsmiths College, London (1978-81). He has had several solo shows, including Ikon Gallery, Birmingham (1988), Todd Gallery, London (1995), Hales Gallery, London (1997), One in the Other, London (1998) and Beaux Art, London (2000). Group exhibitions include *Problems of Picturing*, Serpentine Gallery, London (1984), Aperto Section, Venice Biennale (1990), LandEscapes, Turin (1994) and *The East Wing Exhibition*, Courtauld Gallery, London (1996-98). He was first prize-winner in the *John Moores 19*, Walker Art Gallery, Liverpool (1995), a prize-winner in *John Moores 20*, Walker Art Gallery, Liverpool (1997) and a finalist in the *Jerwood Painting Prize* in 1998. He lives and works in London.

Marysia Lewandowska was born in Szczecin, Poland, in 1955. She studied at Jagiellonian University, Cracow (1974-77) and University of Warsaw (1980). She has lived in London since 1985, and teaches at Goldsmiths College, London. Her recent projects include *Errata*, Louisiana Museum of Modern Art (1996), *Pour Les Curieux*, Musée d'Art et d'Histoire, Geneva (a year-long collaboration with Neil Cummings in 1998) and *Must Go!* on GNER trains for Photo '98. She was also included in *Material Culture*, Hayward Gallery, London (1997). She writes extensively on contemporary visual culture and has edited *Sight Works* since 1988. In 1985 she established the Women's Audio Archive in London.

Brad Lochore was born in Wellington, New Zealand, in 1960. He was educated at Byam Shaw School of Art, London (1986-89), Kunst Akademie, Düsseldorf (1989-90) and Goldsmiths College, London (1990-92). His solo exhibitions have included Base Gallery, Tokyo (1998), Angel Row Gallery, Nottingham (1998) and Victoria Miro Gallery, London (1998). Group exhibitions include *John Moores 19*, Walker Art Gallery, Liverpool (1995), *Visione Britannica 2*, Valentina Moncada, Rome (1999) and *Land and Beauty*, Northern Centre for Contemporary Art, Sunderland (1999). He lives and works in London.

Melanie Manchot was born in Witten, Germany, in 1966. She studied at the International Center of Photography, New York, and New York University (1988-89) before coming to London where she attended City University (1989-90) and Royal College of Art (1990-92). Her recent solo exhibitions include Ffotogallery, Cardiff (1999), Galerie Fiebig, Berlin (1999) and Galerie Hans-Jürgen Siegert, Basel (1999). Group exhibitions have included *Outpost,* Venice Biennale (1995) and *Bankside Browser*, Tate Gallery, London (1999). Her work has been published in a recent monograph, *look at you loving me*, and she is working on a book of new work with Prestel Publishers scheduled for 2000.

Nicholas May was born in Limavady, County Derry, Northern Ireland, in 1962. He attended Bath Academy of Art (1981-84) and Goldsmiths College, London (1988-90). His solo exhibitions include Cornerhouse, Manchester (1994), Victoria Miro Gallery, London (1996), Proposition Gallery, Belfast (1998) and 291 Gallery, London (1998). He has participated in many group exhibitions, including *Visione Britannica*, Valentina Moncada, Rome (1993), *Sense and Sensibility*, Kettle's Yard, Cambridge (1993), *New Painting from the Arts Council Collection*, a National Touring Exhibition from the Hayward Gallery, London (1994-95) and *Host*, Tramway, Glasgow (1997). He lives and works in London.

Ian McLean was born in Hitchin in 1973. He studied at Goldsmiths College, London (1992-96). He has had solo exhibitions at Platform, London (1999) and Christian Dam Galleri, Oslo (1999). His recent group exhibitions include *Heart & Soul*, 60 Long Lane, London (1999) and *Voice Imitator*, Platform, London (1999). He lives and works in London.

Stephen Murphy was born in London in 1962. He studied at St Martins School of Art, London (1984-87) and Goldsmiths College, London (1990-92). Since then he has appeared in various group exhibitions including *Nature Morte*, Tanya Bonakdar Gallery, New York (1994), *Ideal Standard Summer Time*, Lisson Gallery, London (1995) and Mot & Van den Boogard, Brussels (1997). He collaborated with Don Brown at *Turnaround*, Hayward Gallery, London (1996) and had a solo exhibition at 303 Gallery, New York (1999). He lives and works in London.

Mariele Neudecker was born in Düsseldorf in 1965. She attended Goldsmiths College, London (1987-90) and Chelsea School of Art, London (1991-92). Her recent solo exhibitions include *Stolen Sunsets*, Studio Galeria, Budapest (1996), *Unrecallable Now*, Spike Island, Bristol (1998) and James Harris Gallery, Seattle (1999). She was also recently included in Melbourne International Biennial (1999) and *The New Landscape*, British Council tour (2000). She was the MoMart prize-winner at Whitechapel Open, London (1996) and was awarded the First Prize for

biographies

Sculpture at the 7th International Biennial of Sculpture and Drawing, Portugal (1997). She was awarded the Henry Moore Fellowship at Spike Island, Bristol, in 1998, and in the same year was appointed Senior Reseach Fellow in Fine Art, UWIC, Cardiff. She lives and works in Cardiff.

Renato Niemis was born in London in 1958. He studied Physics at Imperial College, London, before studying Fine Art at Harrow College, Camberwell School of Art, London, and Chelsea School of Art, London, where he graduated with an MA in Sculpture in 1992. He has subsequently participated in a number of group exhibitions, notably the *Barclays Young Artist Award* at Serpentine Gallery, London (1993), *A Fête Worse Than Death*, Factual Nonsense, London (1994), Zeppelin Museum, Friedrichshafen (1996) and Die Insel, Germany (1998). His recent solo exhibitions include the Museum of Installation, London (1994), *Spirits in the Machine*, Imperial War Museum, London (1995) and *Slugs and snails and puppy dogs' tails*, Factual Nonsense, London (1996). He lives and works in London.

Jonathan Parsons was born in Redhill in 1970. He attended Goldsmiths College, London (1989-92). He had two solo exhibitions at Richard Salmon Gallery, London (1996, 1999). Recent group exhibitions include *Plastic*, Arnolfini, Bristol (1996), *Pictura Britannica*, British Council tour (1997-98), *Educating Barbie*, Trans Hudson Gallery, New York (1998) and *Furniture*, John Hansard Gallery, Southampton (1999). He lives and works in Farnham.

Gary Perkins was born in Manchester in 1967. He attended Liverpool School of Art (1985-88) and Chelsea School of Art, London (1995-96). In 1998 he was awarded the MoMart Fellowship at Tate Gallery Liverpool. He has had a solo exhibition at Victoria Miro Gallery, London (1996) and his recent group exhibitions include *Within These Walls*, Kettle's Yard, Cambridge (1997), *At One Remove*, Henry Moore Institute, Leeds (1997), *Material Culture*, Hayward Gallery, London (1997), *Pictura Britannica*, British Council tour (1997-98) and *Trace*, Liverpool Biennial of Contemporary Art (1999). He lives and works in London.

Hadrian Pigott was born in Aldershot in 1961. He first studied Geology at Exeter University (1980-83) before going to Royal College of Art, London, to study Sculpture (1990-93). He was a prize-winner in the Whitworth Young Contemporaries in 1993 and he has had solo exhibitions at Jibby Beane, London (1994), Victoria Miro Gallery, London (1998), James van Damme Gallery, Brussels (1998) and Percy Miller, London (1999). He was also included in *Fetishism*, a National Touring Exhibition from the Hayward Gallery, London (1995), *Craft*, Richard Salmon Gallery, London and Kettle's Yard, Cambridge

(1997) and *The Hand*, Power Plant of Contemporary Art, Toronto (1999). He lives and works in London.

Joanna Price was born in Campile, Ireland, in 1956. She studied Philosophy and Ecomonics at University College, London (1976-78) before going to City and Guilds of London Art School (1979-82). She has also studied in Paris and USA. She has had several solo exhibitions at Anna Bornholt Gallery, London, and was included in *John Moores 18*, Walker Art Gallery, Liverpool (1993), *Munich*, Munich Kunstverein (1996) and *Jerwood Painting Prize* (1997). She lives and works in London.

James Rielly was born in Wrexham, Wales, in 1956. He studied at Gloucester College of Art, Cheltenham (1975-78) and Belfast College of Art (1980-81). He was awarded the MoMart Fellowship at Tate Gallery Liverpool in 1995 and has held fellowships at several other institutions including the Künstlerhaus Bethanien, Berlin (1988-89). His solo exhibitions include Musée des Beaux-Arts de Nantes (1997) and Spencer Brownstone Gallery, New York (1999) as well as regular exhibitions at Laurent Delaye Gallery, London, since 1994. He was a prize-winner at *John Moores 19*, Walker Art Gallery, Liverpool (1995) and shortlisted for the *Jerwood Painting Prize* in 1997. He lives and works in London.

Gary Rough was born in Glasgow in 1972. He studied at Glasgow School of Art (1991-95 and 1996-98) and Hochschule der Kunst, Berlin (1997). He was selected as the Scottish Artist in Residence for the Copenhagen European City of Culture in 1996. His solo exhibitions include Inverleith House, Edinburgh (1996) and Jacob Fabricius, Copenhagen (1999). He was also included in *Ideal Standard Summertime*, Lisson Gallery, London, and *Tell Everyone*, Greene Naftali Gallery, New York (both 1995), *Host*, Tramway, Glasgow (1998) and *La Premiere Opening Show*, Galleri Nicolai Wallner, Copenhagen (1999). He lives and works in Glasgow and New York.

Emma Rushton was born in Pickering, North Yorkshire, in 1965. She studied at Brighton Polytechnic (1986-89) and Royal College of Art, London (1990-92). Her work has been exhibited in solo shows at British Council Window Gallery, Prague (1995), L'Observatoire Galerie, Brussels (1996), Bluecoat Gallery, Liverpool (1996), Aspex Gallery, Portsmouth (1996) and Museumsakademie Berlin (1999). Group exhibitions have included *U.K. Wit and Excess*, tour in Australia (1995), *Private View*, Bowes Museum (1996) and *New Art from Britain*, Kunstraum Innsbruck (1998). In 1997-98 Emma Rushton initiated and organised *The Mule*, a newspaper/Internet project, in collaboration with Derek Tyman and Roman Vasseur. She lives and works in London.

biographies

Nina Saunders was born in Odense, Denmark, in 1958. She came to England at the age of seventeen, and studied Fine Art and Critical Studies at Central St Martin's College of Art and Design, London (1986-91). Her solo exhibitions include *Familiar Territories*, Ferens Art Gallery, Hull (1995) and *Hidden Agenda*, Bluecoat Gallery, Liverpool, and the Northern Centre for Contemporary Art, Sunderland (1997). She has participated twice in *Sculpture in the Close* at Jesus College, Cambridge, and was featured in the BBC series *A Date with an Artist* (1997). She lives and works in London.

Jane Simpson was born in London in 1965. She studied at Chelsea School of Art, London (1985-88) and Royal Academy Schools, London (1990-93). Her solo exhibitions include Laurent Delaye Gallery, London (1996), The Approach, London (1998), Norrtälje Konsthall, Sweden (1999) and Asprey Jacques (2000). She was also included in *Some Went Mad, Some Ran Away*, curated by Damien Hirst at Serpentine Gallery, London (1994), *Reternity*, Swedish National Art Museum, Stockholm (1996) and *Here to Stay*, a National Touring Exhibition from the Hayward Gallery, London (1998-99). She lives and works in London.

Kerry Stewart was born in Paisley in 1965. After studying History of Art and German at Edinburgh University (1985-89), she studied Sculpture at Chelsea School of Art, London (1989-93). Her first solo exhibition was at Yorkshire Sculpture Park in 1995. Since then she has had solo exhibitions at Centre of Contemporary Arts, Glasgow (1996), Barbara Thumm, Berlin (1997) and Royal Festival Hall, London (1999), as well as regular showings at Stephen Friedman Gallery, London. Recent group shows include *Belladonna*, Institute of Contemporary Arts, London (1997), *False Impressions*, British School in Rome (1997) and *Pictura Britannica*, British Council tour (1997-98). She lives and works in London.

Marcus Taylor was born in Belfast in 1964. He studied at Ulster Polytechnic (1982-83), Camberwell School of Art (1983-86) and Slade School of Art, London (1986-88). His solo exhibitions include White Cube, London (1993), Kerlin Gallery, Dublin (1994), Berwick Gymnasium Gallery, Northumberland (1996) and the Tannery, London (1998). Recent group exhibitions include *The British Art Show 4*, a National Touring Exhibition from the Hayward Gallery, London (1995-96), *Plastic*, Richard Salmon Gallery, London (1996), *Material Culture*, Hayward Gallery, London (1997) and *Still*, Laurent Delaye, London (1998). He lives and works in London.

Carina Weidle was born in Novo Hamburgo, Brazil, in 1966. She attended the Fine Art School of Parana, Brazil (1985-88) and Goldsmiths College, London (1989-92). She has had solo exhibitions at British Council Building, Prague (1993), Galeria Camargo Vilaça, São Paulo (1996) and Ybakatu Espaço de Arte, Curitiba (1997). She was also included in *Personal Worlds*, Riverside Studios, London (1993), *Thinking Aloud*, Small Mansions, London (1994) and *Panorama da Arte Brasileira*, Museu de Arte Moderna, São Paulo (1996). She lives and works in Curitiba in Brazil.

John Wilkins was born in Colchester in 1951. He studied at St Martins School of Art, London (1971-74) and Royal College of Art, London (1974-77). His recent solo exhibitions include Lugar do Desenho-Fundação Júlio Resende, Gondomar (1998) and Centro de Arte S João da Madeira, Porto (1999), as well as regular showings at Anthony Reynolds Gallery, London. He has also participated in many group exhibitions including *The Pleasure of Aesthetic Life*, The Showroom, London (1996), *John Moores*, Walker Art Gallery, Liverpool (1997, 1999) and *ACE!*, a National Touring Exhibition from the Hayward Gallery, London (1996-97). He lives and works in London.

Richard Wilson was born in London in 1953. He studied at Hornsey College of Art (1971-74) before attending Reading University (1974-76). In 1983 he formed the Bow Gamelan Ensemble (with A. Bean and P. Burwell) and in 1999 he was made a member of the Artistic Records Committee at Imperial War Museum, London. His most recent solo shows include *Jamming Gears*, Serpentine Gallery, London (1996), *Irons in the Fire*, Globe Gallery, South Shields (1998) and *Hung Drawn and Quartered* at Stadtisches Museum, Zwickau and Ha'umche Gallery, Tel Aviv (1998, 1999). He also made the *North Meadow Sculpture Project* at the Millennium Dome. He lives and works in London.

Lucy Wood was born in Slough in 1969. She studied at Camberwell School of Art, London (1989-92) and then completed an MA in Arts Criticism at City University, London (1992-94). She was included in *Tracer*, the Tannery, London (1996) and *Playing Dead*, Spacex Gallery, Exeter (1997), *Whitechapel Open*, London (1997), *East International*, Norwich (1998) and *Dumbfounded*, Battersea Arts Centre, London (1999). She lives and works in London.

Richard Woods was born in Cheshire in 1966. He studied at Winchester School of Fine Art (1985-88) and Slade School of Art, London (1988-90). He has had solo exhibitions at Winchester Gallery (1993), Hales Gallery, London (1994) and Galerie 'M', Stockholm (1997) and ART DK, Copenhagen (1998). He has been included in many group exhibitions including *At One Remove*, Henry Moore Institute, Leeds (1997), *New York Drawers*, Brooklyn Museum, New York and Cornerhouse, Manchester (1997) and *Interactive*, Amerada Hess, London (1998). He lives and works in London.

biographies

British Art Show 5, exhibition catalogue, Hayward Gallery Publishing, London, 2000

Brooks Adams, Lisa Jardine, Martin Maloney, Norman Rosenthal, Richard Shone, **Sensation: Young British Artists from the Saatchi Collection**, Royal Academy of Arts, London, 1997. [Richard Billingham, Glenn Brown, Simon Callery, Adam Chodzko, Keith Coventry, Paul Finnegan, Mark Francis, Alex Hartley, Abigail Lane, Langlands & Bell, Jonathan Parsons, Hadrian Pigott, James Rielly, Jane Simpson]

Louisa Buck, **Moving Targets: A User's Guide to British Art Now**, Tate Gallery Publishing, London, 1997

David Burrows (ed.), **Who's Afraid of Red White & Blue?**, ARTicle Press, Birmingham, 1998

Matthew Collings, **Blimey! From Bohemia to Britpop**, 21 Publishing, London, 1997

Matthew Collings, **This is Modern Art**, Weidenfeld & Nicolson, London, 1999

Richard Cork, Rose Finn-Kelcey, Thomas Lawson, **The British Art Show 4**, Hayward Gallery Publishing, London, 1995. [Jordan Baseman, John Frankland, Kerry Stewart, Marcus Taylor]

Douglas Fogle, **Brilliant! New Art from London**, Walker Art Center, Minneapolis, 1996. [Glenn Brown, Adam Chodzko, Abigail Lane]

Ann Gallagher, **Dimensions Variable**, The British Council, London, 1997. [Martin Creed, Graham Gussin, Stephen Murphy]

Andrew Graham-Dixon, **Broken English**, Serpentine Gallery, London, 1991

Sarah Kent, **Young British Artists I-VI**, The Saatchi Gallery, London, 1992-96. [I: John Greenwood, Langlands & Bell; II: Rose Finn-Kelcey; III: Simon Callery, Simon English; IV: John Frankland, Brad Lochore, Marcus Taylor; V: Glenn Brown, Keith Coventry, Hadrian Pigott, Kerry Stewart; VI: Jordan Baseman, Daniel Coombs, Claude Heath, John Isaacs, Nina Saunders]

Sarah Kent, **Shark Infested Waters: The Saatchi Collection of British Art in the 90s**, Zwemmer, London, 1994. [Glenn Brown, Simon Callery, Rod Dickinson, Katharine Dowson, Simon English, Rose Finn-Kelcey, John Frankland, John Greenwood, Alex Hartley, Abigail Lane, Langlands & Bell, David Leapman, Brad Lochore, Stephen Murphy, Renato Niemis, Hadrian Pigott, Joanna Price, Emma Rushton, Jane Simpson, Kerry Stewart, Marcus Taylor, Carina Weidle, John Wilkins, Richard Wilson]

Sarah Kent, Richard Cork, Dick Price, **Young British Art: The Saatchi Decade**, Booth Clibborn Editions, London, 1999. [Liz Arnold, Alan Ball, Jordan Baseman, Richard Billingham, Terence Bond, Martin Boyce, Glenn Brown, Simon Callery, Adam Chodzko, Daniel Coombs, Keith Coventry, Rod Dickinson, Simon English, Paul Finnegan, Rose Finn-Kelcey, Mark Francis, John Frankland, Alison Gill, John Greenwood, Siobhán Hapaska, Alex Hartley, Claude Heath, Nicky Hirst, Louise Hopkins, John Isaacs, Chantal Joffe, Darren Lago, Abigail Lane, Langlands & Bell, David Leapman, Brad Lochore, Melanie Manchot, Nicholas May, Stephen Murphy, Mariele Neudecker, Renato Niemis, Jonathan Parsons, Gary Perkins, Hadrian Pigott, Joanna Price, James Rielly, Emma Rushton, Nina Saunders, Jane Simpson, Kerry Stewart, Marcus Taylor, Carina Weidle, Richard Wilson, Lucy Wood, Richard Woods]

Susan May, **Here to Stay: Arts Council Collection Purchases of the 1990s**, Hayward Gallery Publishing, London, 1998. [Richard Billingham, Siobhán Hapaska, Mariele Neudecker, Hadrian Pigott, Jane Simpson, Kerry Stewart, Richard Woods]

Gregor Muir, James Roberts, **General Release**, The British Council, London, 1995

Bernice Murphy, Patricia Bickers, Stephen Snoddy et al., **Pictura Britannica: Art from Britain**, The British Council, London, 1997. [Jordan Baseman, Richard Billingham, John Frankland, Louise Hopkins, Jonathan Parsons, Gary Perkins, Kerry Stewart]

Dick Price, **The New Neurotic Realism**, The Saatchi Gallery, London, 1998. [Chantal Joffe]

Artists who are included in *The Saatchi Gift to the Arts Council Collection* are noted in square brackets.